All That Glitters:

The Men and Women of the Gold and Silver Rushes

Edited by Phyllis Raybin Emert

Discovery Enterpris
Lowell, Massachι

© Discovery Enterprises, Ltd., Lowell, MA 1995
ISBN 1-878668-49-8 paperback edition
Library of Congress Catalog Card Number 94-69885

10   9   8   7   6   5   4   3   2

Printed in the United States of America

Dedication

For Matt Emert and Larry Emert

Special thanks to:

The Libraries of the Claremont Colleges, Claremont, California
Andrea Tarr, Reference Librarian

Subject Reference Guide

All That Glitters:
The Men and Women of the Gold and Silver Rushes
edited by Phyllis Raybin Emert

Gold and Silver Rushes — Juvenile Literature

The West — Juvenile Literature

American History — Juvenile Literature

Photo/Illustration Credits

Cover and page 28:

Renderings by Jeffrey D. Pollock, based on watercolor
paintings of a miner panning for gold and a sluice miner,
by O.C. Seltzer, Thomas Gilcrease Institute,
Tulsa, Oklahoma.

Title page and page 28: Library of Congress
Page 36: Wells Fargo Bank
Page 39: Harpers

Table of Contents

Overview
by Phyllis Raybin Emert

The gold and silver rushes of the middle to late 19th century changed the United States in a number of significant ways. When gold was discovered in 1848, the states of Missouri, Iowa, and Texas made up the western boundary of the country. Travel farther west and one encountered an essentially uncivilized wilderness of regions and territories, populated by a variety of Indian tribes, immigrants, settlers, and exotic buffalo.

The discovery of gold, first in California, then in the regions of Colorado and Nevada, followed by major silver strikes in these areas, stimulated an extraordinary amount of economic growth. Efforts to meet the needs of the miners and other people who migrated to the West in droves led to unrivaled progress and expansion in the fields of agriculture, commerce, transportation, and industry.

As the population increased, so did the formation of towns, cities, and local governmental administrations. The need for law and order evolved into an organized criminal justice system. This combination led to the eventual achievement of statehood, and, by the turn of the century, the continental United States was much as it is today.*

*The exceptions were Arizona and New Mexico, both admitted to the Union in 1912.

In The Beginning

In 1839, a Swiss immigrant named John Augustus Sutter arived in California. He acquired a land grant from the Mexican government (which owned the territory at the time) where the Sacramento and American Rivers came together. Sutter built a trading post and had plans to erect a sawmill. He called the area New Helvetia.

Everyone referred to the adobe walled building as "Sutter's Fort." Its walls were 18 feet high and cannons were mounted at two of the corners. Many travelers stopped by Sutter's Fort as a resting place before heading east across the territories to the United States, north to Oregon, or west to the little settlement of Yerba Buena near the Pacific coast.

In December 1845, the United States, in a formal act of annexation, assumed control over the Mexican-owned territory of Texas. This angered the Mexicans and when President James K. Polk attempted to purchase New Mexico and California, the Mexican government refused to negotiate. War broke out between the two countries in 1846.

The United States was victorious and the Treaty of Guadalupe Hidalgo was officially signed on February 2, 1848. Mexico was forced to give up California and New Mexico and recognized the Rio Grande River as the border of Texas.

California was now United States territory. One of the first things the residents of Yerba Buena did was to rename their settlement San Francisco. Meanwhile, John Sutter and his new partner, James Marshall, were busy building a sawmill on the South Fork of the American River.

Gold Is Discovered!

What happened next changed the course of American history and influenced the lives of nearly every American in one way or another. One of those affected was eighteen-year-old Azariah Smith. He was a volunteer with the Mormon battalion in the American Army of the West, which was assigned to fight the Mexican forces in New Mexico and California during the war. They were directed to open a supply line from Santa Fe to American troops in San Diego. By the time the Mormon Battalion arrived on the west coast, the final battles of the war had been over for several weeks.

Smith became part of the occupying army and the battalion was soon released from service. Groups of Mormons headed north to Sutter's Fort where they planned to travel eastward to the area around Salt Lake.

By now it was late January of 1848 and Sutter and Marshall began hiring workers to build their sawmill. Azariah Smith and his friends decided to earn some additional money before beginning their long journey, and signed on with Sutter.

The following excerpts describe the discovery of gold in California by eyewitness Smith and Edward Gould Buffum, a Quaker who was among the first wave of argonauts, the term for those who flocked to California to search for gold in 1848-9. (The original spelling and grammar have been left as they were originally written.)

The Gold Discovery Journal of Azariah Smith

by Azariah Smith

(Edited by Bigler, Salt Lake City, Utah: University of Utah Press, 1990, pp. 108-112, 115)

Sunday Jan. the 30th 48. Mr. Marshall haveing arived we got liberty of him, and built a small house down by the mill, and last Sunday we moved into it...This week Mon. the 24th Mr. Marshall found some pieces of (as we all suppose) Gold, and he has gone to the Fort, for the purpose of finding out. It is found in the raceway [the bed or channel of a river or stream] in small pieces; some have been found that would weigh five dollars.

Sunday Febuary the 6th. Mr. Marshall has returned with the fact that it is Gold; and Captain Sutter came here Wednesday with Johnston, for the purpose of looking at the mine, where the Gold is found, and got enough for a ring. The captain brought us a bottle of Liquor, and some pocket knives...

Monday Feb. the 14th. The past week I did not work but three days and a half. Mr. Marshall grants us the privelege of picking up Gold odd spells and Sundays, and I have gathered up considerable...

Tuesday March the 28th. Last Sunday I with three others went [down] the river on the other side and picked up considerable Gold. Yest[erday] I received a letter from Father, which pleases me much. He said that [he] arived at the Salt Lake, Oct the 27th. 1847. and had good luck except the loss of one horse.

Friday April the 7th... Mr. Marshall has gave us the privelige [of] hunting Gold and haveing half we find, and we are a going [to take] the opportunity. I have something like thirty dollars of [gold].

Friday May the 26th...on Thursday the 11th. we went up, [to the gold mine] and stayed there until Tuesday the 23rd., when we came down.

While there we had very good luck; I got there something near three hundred dollars, which makes me in all some upwards of four hundred dollars. The most I made in a day was sixty five dollars after the toll was taken out, which was thirty dollars out of a hundred, which goes to Hudson and Willis, that discovered the mine, and Brannon who is securing it for them. Before we came away, men, women and children, from the Bay and other places in California, were flocking to the gold mine, by the dozens, and by wagon loads.

Six Months In The Gold Mines

by E. Gould Buffum

(Edited by Caughey, The Ward Ritchie Press, 1959, originally published in 1850, pp. 50-52)

One morning Marshall...discovered, much to his astonishment, some small shining particles in the sand at the bottom of the race, which upon examination he became satisfied were gold...Of course, the news spread like wild fire, and in less than one week after the news reached Monterey, one thousand people were on their way to the gold region...Before the middle of July, the whole lower country was depopulated. Rancheros left their herds to revel in delightful liberty upon the hills of their ranchos; merchants closed their stores, lawyers left their clients, doctors their patients, soldiers took "French leave."

Colonel Mason, then Governor of California, was himself seized with the "mania." and taking his adjutant and an escort, started for the mines, "in order to be better able to make a report to the Government..." Every idler in the country, who could purchase, beg, or steal, a horse, was off, and ere the first of August the principal towns were entirely deserted...

Hundreds and sometimes even thousands of dollars were spoken of as the reward of a day's labour...In the mean time, new discoveries had been made at Mormon Island, as far north as the Yuba River, and as far south as the Stanislaus; and the mining population had swelled to about three thousand. The stories that had been put in circulation in regard to the richness of the placers [deposits of sand and gravel usually in water containing gold and other minerals] were in the main true. A few months after their discovery I saw men, in whom I placed the utmost confidence, who assured me that for days in succession they had dug from the bowels of the earth over five hundred dollars a day.

By September of 1848, the gold discovery in California was on everyone's lips throughout the country and even in Europe. When President Polk confirmed the gold strike in his annual message to Congress on December 5, 1848, the country went wild and the gold rush had begun.

Journeys West

There were two main reasons why so many risked so much to travel so far. The first was the possibility of instant wealth; the second, the search for adventure. According to Helen S. Giffen in her introduction to *The Peter Decker Diaries,* "[For] a young man with few financial attachments, and with a youthful hankering for adventure, it is not surprising that the news of the gold discovery in California should stir in him the desire to be up and away and to try his fortune in a new country."

The expression, "going to see the elephant," was popularly used to refer to those who participated in the California gold rush. "For gold rushers," explained Joann Levy in her book, *They Saw The Elephant,* "the elephant symbolized both the high cost of their endeavor—the myriad possibilities for misfortune on the journey or in California—and...an exotic sight, an unequaled experience, the adventure of a lifetime."

By 1850 about 200,000 people had left the security of their homes, friends, and families to journey west. Although most were single males, many married men were accompanied by wives and children.

By Sea

Routes by sea were available from most Atlantic Ocean ports. Some chose the long voyage around Cape Horn and through the Straits of Magellan at the tip of South America. Severe storms often affected ships which traveled this route. Elizabeth Gunn wrote about her sea voyage in 1851, "A gale commenced on Tuesday at noon and lasted till Friday, and we were tossed about in fine order. We could neither stand nor sit and of course must lie down…"

Many traveled by ship to Panama or Nicaragua, then overland to a Pacific Ocean port. Others journeyed by ship to Vera Cruz, then overland to Acapulco on the Pacific coast of Mexico.

Mary Jane Megquier (pronounced Me-Gweer) accompanied her husband, Dr. Thomas Lewis Megquier of Winthrop, Maine, to California in 1849. The following excerpts are from letters written to her children, friends, and relatives which described the sea voyage via the Panama route.

✧✧✧✧✧

Apron Full Of Gold

by Mary Jane Megquier

(Edited by Cleland, The Huntington Library, San Marino, CA: 1949, pp. 8-10, 15-17, 22-24)

March 13, 1849

DEAR ANGE …The first day of March we sailed from N.Y. in the splendid steamship Northerner, we had a fine northeast storm for three days, we were obliged to go two or three hundred miles out of our course, which has made our journey some longer but since that, we have had a succession of the finest weather you ever knew…I have enjoyed it much better than I expected, there is about two hundred gentlemen and I am the only lady and in that case I receive every attention…

Panama, April 22

The demand is so great, provisions are enormously high—flour $50. a barrel, codfish 25 cents per pound, ham 50, and other things in proportion. The Americans are pouring in from all parts of the States, notwithstanding they have been written to, that is very difficult to get a passage. Their thirst for gold is such, they

12

start without a ticket or the means of getting a passage in a sailing vessel when they arrive here. They will gamble, thinking to add to their little stock and lose their last dollar. There is supposed to be about two thousand Americans here; every nook and corner is filled; many of them I think would not be recognized by their friends; they let their hair and beards grow, wear a red shirt and a pair of overalls and a slouched hat, looking less like civilization then the natives...the Oregon which has made one trip to San Francisco and brings great news from there, the passengers that came in her, are all loaded with gold, but they have to endure many hardships, and it is almost impossible to get a shelter for your head, but womens help is so very scarce that I am in hopes to get a chance by hook or crook to pay my way...a woman that can work will make more money than a man, and I think now that I shall do that which will bring in the most change, for the quicker the money is made the sooner we shall meet...They tell us our expenses will be as high again in S.F. not of scarcity of provision but of help, every body is digging gold, even the cabin boy has his thousands, they get in big lumps, one passed through this place weighing thirty six ounces pure gold. What think of that? In about one year you will see your Mother come trudging home with an apron full, but without joking, gold is very plenty and if I do not like we shall get it as fast as possible and start for home...

ᔥᔥᔥᔥᔥᔥᔥᔥ

San Francisco, June 18.49.

DEAR DAUGHTER I wrote you from Panama when we were to start for this place, which we did according to our expectations. At three o'clock we went aboard raining as fast as it could pour, found about four hundred passengers five ladies and two servants...For the first two days I was quite seasick but I did not suffer so much from that, as from the heat, for the first

13

Billboards in Boston and New York advertised trips to California.

14

two weeks I came near being roasted alive, after that it was impossible to keep warm, the gentlemen put on two overcoats and then they were as blue as pigeons. The first port we put into was Acapulco...the next stopping place was San Blas... Our next port was San Diego...Our last stopping place was Monterey...report says there are six thousand people here that have no shelter, but some are going and coming from the mines, so we got a small room the size of my bed room in Winthrop for five of us with our luggage...

By Land

There were several ways to get to California by land, but these routes were only possible in the spring and summer months when the mountains were free of snow and storms.

Some travelers took the Santa Fe Trail to the Gila River and through the Sonora desert. But most took the central route from either Independence, Missouri, St. Joseph, Missouri, or Council Bluffs, Iowa, along the Platte, North Platte, and Sweetwater Rivers, and through the South Pass over the Rockies. There they had the choice of several different routes (Carson River, Truckee River, or Lassen Cut-off) which finally led them across the Sierra Nevada Mountains to California.

The overland journey was a long and difficult one, and great hardships were endured by both the people and their animals. Overlanders had to deal with disease, terrible heat or extreme cold, fatigue, and oftentimes a lack of food and water.

Many wrote of their experiences in diaries and journals. The following men and women, though different in background, age, education, and skills, had one major thing in common, which drove them on, sometimes against impossible odds — their thirst for gold.

A Frontier Lady

by Sarah Royce

(Edited by Gabriel, New Haven, CT: Yale University Press, 1960, originally published in 1932, pp. 3, 5, 34)

On the last day of April, 1849 we began our journey to California. Our out-fit consisted of a covered wagon, well loaded with provisions, and such preparations for sleeping, cooking etc., as we had been able to furnish, guided only by the light of Fremont's *Travels*, and the suggestions, often conflicting, of the many who, like ourselves, utter strangers to camping life, were setting out for the "Golden Gate." Our wagon was drawn by three yoke of oxen and one yoke of cows, the latter being used in the team only part of the time. Their milk was of course to be a valuable part of our subsistence...

It soon became plain that the hard facts of this pilgrimage would require patience, energy, and courage fully equal to what I had anticipated when I had tried to stretch my imagination to the utmost...Deep mud-holes in which the wagon would stick fast, or, still worse, sloughs...covered with turf that appeared perfectly sound, but which would break when the full weight came upon it, and let the wheels in nearly to the hubs; closing round the spokes so tightly that digging, alone, would free them. In these cases, the whole, or nearly the whole, of the contents of the wagon had to be unloaded, often in very miry places sometimes in the rain, while the men had to "put shoulder to the wheels" and lift them out by main force. Several times while we were all busy, in such a scene the cattle wandered off, into a wood or over a hill, and hours would be lost in getting them together...

Our only guide from Salt Lake City consisted of two small sheets of note paper, sewed together, and bearing on the outside in writing the title, 'Best Guide to the Gold Mines, 816 miles, by Ira Willes, GSL City.'

This little pamphlet was wholly in writing, there being at that time no printing press at Salt Lake. It was gotten up by a man who had been to California and back the preceding year. The directions, and the descriptions of camping places, together with the distances seemed pretty definite and satisfactory until they reached the lower part of the Mary's or Humboldt River; when poor camping and scarcity of water were mentioned with discouraging frequency. From the sink of the Humboldt, all seemed confusion...

Scharmann's Overland Journey To California

by H.B. Scharmann

(Translated by Zimmermann and Zimmermann, Freeport, NY: Books for Libraries Press, 1969, originally published in 1918, pp. 13, 26, 29, 31-32, 34)

This overland journey is one of the most unfortunate undertakings to which man may allow himself to be lured, because he cannot possibly have any conception before starting of this kind of travelling. To be sure, there is a beaten path which you see clearly before you, but there are no stopping-places with even the slightest signs of civilization. Everyone is going and no one is coming back. You leave your camp in the hope of finding water, and a grazing place for the cattle a few miles further on; but sometimes it happens that you are forced to halt in a place where neither grass nor water can be found. This means intense suffering for the cattle and often an irretrievable loss...

17

The land...from Fort Laramie to California is not worth a cent, I think. It consists of nothing but desert-land and bare mountains covered with boulders and red soil which makes them resemble volcanoes. The best thing the traveller can do is to hurry on as fast as possible from one river to the other...

As soon as we left the Humboldt River we came into a desert, seventy miles wide, although it had been represented to us as only thirty. Wells had been dug in the midst of this desert, but nowhere was there any grass for the cattle. During the day we rested, and at night, when it became a little cooler, we drove on. Even though we exerted all our strength, we took a day and two nights to cross the first part of the desert, where nothing but volcanic mountains on all sides could be seen. We had to travel thirty-three miles more before we could regard our cattle as saved. The heat was oppressive and clouds of alkaline dust enveloped us. I examined the soil and found it to consist of a mixture of salt, chalk and ashes. Both in front and in back of us was a long train of wagons, so that at least I had company in my misery. Now we came to a place where we saw a neatly arranged row of wagons. All of them were empty and abandoned. In order to save as much as possible, the owners had unharnessed the cattle and had driven them on rapidly. Those who had no families took their bundles on their shoulders and proceeded on foot. The families were all the more to be pitied.

...My whole water supply barely sufficed to make a cup of tea or coffee for my wife. This was our whole supper. On the road over which I had travelled during the day I had counted eighty-one shattered and abandoned wagons, and 1,663 oxen, either dead or dying, but no mules.

...The night was calm and quiet. We had gone on about seven miles; I was walking behind the wagon which was moving more slowly every minute. My son halted and joined his mother, who was weeping, mingling his tears with hers. The two leading oxen had lost their last ounce of strength and fell down...

I stood still for a few minutes, pondering and asking myself what could be done in this moment of dire distress. There was no longer any hope for the exhausted oxen. I have often seen these poor animals still alive when wagons, coming after, drove over them. I did not want my oxen to share this fate, so, obeying my wish, my travelling companion took out his gun and freed them from their last struggle. With a heavy heart I continued the journey...

Up to this point we had all experienced some of the illnesses that are inevitable to such a trip. The most common are dysentery, intermittent fever, cholera, and scurvy, all of which are the result of the unhealthful food and water, especially the latter, besides the change of climate. Often we suffered all day from the terrific heat, while the night was so cold that a three- or four - inch layer of ice covered the ground in the morning...

They Saw The Elephant

by Joann Levy

(Hamden, CT: Archon Books, 1990, pp. 6, 7, 16, 17, 19, 20, 21, 73)

We again met with the sick woman...She said her husband had just died of cholera...About an hour after a man rode past us and informed us that she was almost dead then, and that the men in whose company she was were stopping to dig her grave, before she was dead! There's humanity on the Plains! — *Lucy Cooke, 1852*

꒰ᵔ꒱꒰ᵔ꒱꒰ᵔ꒱꒰ᵔ꒱

Away from the river, the soil is hard and dry, void of any vegetation except sage-brush...Much of the level land of this valley is barren, from the salt and alkali in it...The dust is intolerable. Many wear silk handkerchiefs over their faces; others wear goggles. It is a strange-looking army. — *Margaret Frink, 1850*

꒰ᵔ꒱꒰ᵔ꒱꒰ᵔ꒱꒰ᵔ꒱

...The weary journey last night, the mooing of the cattle for water, their exhausted condition, with the cry of 'Another ox down,' the stopping of the train to unyoke the poor dying brute, to let him follow at will or stop by the wayside and die, and the weary, weary tramp of men and beasts, worn out with heat and famished for water, will never be erased from my memory. Just at dawn, in the distance, we had a glimpse of the Truckee River, and with it the feeding: Saved at last! — *Sallie Hester, 1849*

꒰ᵔ꒱꒰ᵔ꒱꒰ᵔ꒱꒰ᵔ꒱

...Horses, mules, and oxen, suffering from heat, thirst, and starvation, staggered along until they fell and died on every rod of the way. Both sides of the road for miles were lined with dead animals and abandoned wagons. Around them were strewed yokes, chains, harness, guns, tools, bedding, clothing-utensils, and many other articles, in utter confusion. The owners had left everything, except what provisions they could carry on their backs, and hurried on to save themselves...But no one stopped to gaze or help. The living procession marched steadily onward, giving little heed to the destruction going on, in their own anxiety to reach a place of safety. In fact, the situation was so desperate that, in most cases, no one could help another. Each had all he could do to save himself and his animals. — *Margaret Fink, 1850*

We halted a day to bury her and the infant that had lived but an hour, in this weird, lonely spot on God's footstool away apparently from everywhere and everybody.

The bodies were wrapped together in a bedcomforter and wound, quite mummyfied with a few yards of string that we made by tying together torn strips of a cotton dress skirt. A passage of the Bible (my own) was read; a prayer offered and 'Nearer, My God to Thee' sung...Every heart was touched and eyes full of tears as we lowered the body, coffinless, into the grave. There was no tombstone — why should there be — the poor husband and orphans could never hope to revisit the grave and to the world it was just one of the many hundreds that marked the trail of the argonaut. — *Catherine Haun, 1849*

✧✧✧✧✧

California Emigrant Letters

by Walker D. Wyman

(New York: Bookman Associates, 1952, originally published in mid-19th century newspapers, pp. 88-90, 123-124)

Sutter's Fort, Jan. 24, 1850

I do not advise any man to come, rich or poor, but to those who will come, I can give them a little advise, especially if they come by land. Ox teams are allowed by all, or nearly so, to be much the surest teams. But the load and the wagon must be properly adjusted to the team...To each man 125 pounds of bacon and 125 pounds of flour is an abundance. One half of his bacon had better be in hams, for the sake of his health; it is much better to eat on the road. The emigrant ought to eat as little greasy food as possible to keep off the scurvy. Risen bread is much better than lard...A plenty of pickles, 1/4 bushel of onions, and 1/2 bushel of beans to each man, is not too much. Vinegar should be used every day.

Apples and peach fruit and rice are useful articles of food as can possibly be taken on the road. To each man 80 pounds of rice, and three quarters of a bushel of apple or peach fruit, at least are necessary, being easily cooked, they are always convenient...
— *"M.M.," to Chambers and Knapp, Missouri* Republican, *Mar. 22, 1850*

෬෬෬෬෬෬෬෬

California, Nov. 10, 1850

...The last of the desert is exceedingly difficult to travel in on account of the great depth and heat of the sand. When we crossed it there was about 100 dead horses on it, and any quantity of wagons, gear, clothing and property of every description. I am informed by others who have lately come in, that it was now estimated that there were 4,000 horses and 2,000 wagons; another told me there were enough dead horses, to put them touching, to line the road from one side of the desert to the other side, and enough wagons to line it on the other; and that the smell arising from the dead horses was so bad the road could not be travelled...

We started from Independence the 29th of April, and reached the first diggings the 29th of July, making the trip in 92 days. The road was measured and made 2100 miles from Council Bluffs, to Weavertown, the first mines, and fifty miles from there to the Sacramento; then if you count the distance you have to go off the route to hunt grass, you may set down the distance at fully 2,500 miles. — *A.M. Williams, to his father, Missouri* Courier, *quoted by the St. Joseph* Adventure, *Feb. 21, 1851*

Diary Of A Forty-Niner

by Alfred T. Jackson

(Edited by Canfield, New York: Turtle Point Press, 1992, originally published in 1906, pp. 58-59)

...I found them camped about eight miles up the ridge and they were certainly in a bad fix. There were three families, men and their wives and five children, one a baby not a month old that had been born on the Humboldt desert. The mother was nothing but skin and bone, a young woman, and she could scarcely walk she was so weak and worn out. It was pitiful to see her cling to and try to nurse the baby, so forlorn that the sight would have melted a heart of stone. The rest of them did not look much better and one, a young girl fourteen years old, was sick to the point of death. They had four yoke of oxen, who were walking skeletons, and, to look at them, it was a miracle that they had succeeded in crossing the mountains, as they were in deep snow all the way until they reached their last camping ground, where they had got out of it and in a place where there was some grass feed for their cattle. Their grub had given out and they did not have enough provisions on hand for another meal. It was one of the saddest plights I ever saw, but I cheered them up and told them they need not worry any more as there would be plenty for them all before sundown. Sure enough, Pard, Lawyer Dunn and Tom Buckner rode into the camp before dark, driving a pack-mule loaded with all kinds of grub. It wasn't long before a good hot meal was prepared; there were willing cooks, and we assured the emigrants that their troubles were over. The poor girl was too sick to eat; in fact was almost unconscious. Her sufferings were too much for Buckner and he swore he would have a doctor there by midnight, if he had to bind him hand and foot and bring him by main force. Buckner is a good fellow if he is a gambler and we knew he would keep his word. The girl's mother coaxed her to swallow a couple of spoonfuls of brandy — Frank Dunn luckily had brought a flask along — and that seemed to revive her. They all felt better after the meal and we built up a big camp fire and set around it listening to the story of their adventures and hardships until Tom got back. Sure enough, he brought Dr. Hunt along with him, who after examining the girl said that it was a case of exhaustion and prostration for want of proper nourishment and that the brandy we had given her was exactly what she needed. Her father broke down completely and sobbed like a child when the doctor told him there was a chance for her recovery. We left them in good spirits, promising to send them up some more grub the next day. Pard advised them to stay where they were for two or three days, until their oxen recruited, and then to come into town and we would see that they got a fair start. This is a land of plenty, but the snowline and starvation is not very far away…

Tools Of The Trade

In the early days of the California gold rush, all a miner needed was a pickax, a pan, and a stream of water to be a pros--pector. This was referred to as placer mining. The water would clean the dirt from the stream-bed out of the pan, leaving the heavier gold flakes and nuggets at the bottom.

According to Robert Wallace in *The Miners*, "gold was unmistakable to anyone who had hefted it and clenched a bit of it between his teeth. Soft and malleable in its pure 24-carat form, gold was the only yellow metal that would not break when it was vigorously pounded or bent..."

The richest placers were found in foothill streams at the base of mountain ranges. Gold was likely to collect in ridges and holes of stream-beds or in gravel, sand, clay banks (called bars) which were often located in the bends of a river.

Time passed and gold was discovered in Colorado and Nevada in 1859, Montana in 1862, the Dakotas in 1876, Colorado again in 1890, as well as other areas. More sophisticated and efficient techniques and equipment came into use in the mining of gold. Instead of pans, miners used rockers, then Long Toms to increase production. Others sank holes directly into the bed-rock to find the richer deposits of gold. Some dammed up streams and rivers, and constructed separate waterways called races. They built wooden flumes to carry water to sites where the earth needed washing. The following excerpts, written by eyewitnesses to the gold rush, describe the various processes and equipment utilized by miners.

Six Months In The Gold Mines

by E. Gould Buffum

(Edited by Caughey, The Ward Ritchie Press, 1959, originally published in 1850, from pages 36-38)

...The apparatus...which has always been the favourite assistant of the gold-digger, was the common rocker or cradle, constructed in the simplest manner. It consists of nothing more than a wooden box or hollowed log, two sides and one end of which are closed, while the other end is left open. At the end which is closed and called the 'mouth' of the machine, a sieve, usually made of a plate of sheet iron, or a piece of raw hide, perforated with holes about half an inch in diameter, is rested upon the sides. A number of 'bars' or 'rifflers' which are little pieces of board from one to two inches in height, are nailed to the bottom, and extend laterally across it. Of these, there are three or four in the machine, and one at the 'tail,' as it is called, i.e. the end where the dirt is washed out. This with a pair of rockers like those of a child's cradle, and a handle to rock it with, complete the description of the machine, which being placed with the rockers upon two logs, and the 'mouth' elevated at a slight angle above the tail, is ready for operation. Modified and improved as this may be, and as in fact it already has been, so long as manual labour is employed for washing gold, the 'cradle' is the best agent to use for that purpose...

The Shirley Letters From The California Mines

by Louise Clappe

(New York: Alfred A. Knopf, 1949, originally published in 1854-55, pp. 132-136)

1852...Here in the mountains, the labor of excavation is extremely difficult, on account of the immense rocks which form a large portion of the soil...In many places the surface-soil, or in mining phrase, the 'top dirt,' 'pays' when worked in a 'Long Tom.' This machine...is a trough, generally about twenty feet in length, and eight inches in depth, formed of wood, with the exception of six feet at one end, called the 'riddle,'...which is made of sheet iron, perforated with holes about the size of a large marble. Underneath this cullender-like portion of the 'long-tom,' is placed another trough, about ten feet long, the sides six inches perhaps in height, which divided through the middle by a slender slat, is called the 'riffle-box.' It takes several persons to manage, properly, a 'long-tom.' Three or four men station themselves with spades, at the head of the machine, while at the foot of it, stands an individual armed 'wid de shovel and de hoe.' The spadesmen throw in large quantities of the precious dirt, which is washing down to the 'riddle' by a stream of water leading into the 'long-tom' through wooden gutters or 'sluices.' When the soil reaches the 'riddle,' it is kept constantly in motion by the man with the hoe. Of course, by this means, all the dirt and gold escapes through the perforations into the 'riffle-box' below, one compartment of which is placed just beyond the 'riddle.' Most of the dirt washes over the sides of the 'riffle-box,' but the gold being so astonishly heavy remains safely at the bottom of it.

27

Rendering of a miner at the "Long Tom", by Jeffrey D. Pollock, based on a water color painting from the Thomas Gilcrease Institute in Tulsa, Oklahoma.

When the machine gets too full of stones to be worked easily, the man whose business it is to attend to them throws them out with his shovel, looking carefully among them as he does so for any pieces of gold, which may have been too large to pass through the holes of the 'riddle.' I am sorry to say that he generally loses his labor. At night they 'pan out' the gold, which has been collected in the 'riffle-box' during the day. Many of the miners decline washing the 'top dirt' at all, but try to reach as quickly as possible the 'bed-rock,' where are found the richest deposits of gold. The river is supposed to have formerly flowed over this 'bed-rock,' in the 'crevices' of which, it left, as it passed away, the largest portions of the so eagerly sought for ore. The group of mountains amidst which we are living is a spur of the Sierra Nevada; and the 'bed-rock,' (which is in this vicinity of slate) is said to run through the entire range, lying, in distance varying from a few feet to eighty or ninety, beneath the surface of the soil. On Indian Bar, the 'bed-rock' falls in almost perpendicular 'benches,' while at Rich Bar, the friction of the river has formed it into large, deep basins, in which the gold, instead of being found, as you would naturally suppose, in the bottom of it, lies for the most part, just below the rim...

When a company wish to reach the bed rock as quickly as possible, they 'sink a shaft,' (which is nothing more nor less than digging a well,) until they 'strike' it. They then commence 'drifting coyote holes' (as they call them) in search of 'crevices,' which, as I told you before, often pay immensely. These 'coyote holes' sometimes extend hundreds of feet into the side of the hill. Of course they are obliged to use lights in working them. They generally proceed, until the air is so impure as to extinguish the lights, when they return to the entrance of the excavation, and commence another, perhaps close to it. When they think that a 'coyote hole' has been faithfully 'worked,' they 'clean it up,' which is done by scraping the surface of the 'bed-rock' with a knife, — lest by chance they have overlooked a 'crevice,' — and they are often richly rewarded for this precaution.

Now I must tell you how those having 'claims' on the hills procure the water for washing them. The expense of raising it in any way from the river, is too enormous to be thought of for a moment. In most cases it is brought from ravines in the mountains. A company, to which a friend of ours belongs, has dug a ditch about a foot in width and depth, and more than three miles length, which is fed in this way. I wish that you could see this ditch. I never beheld a natural streamlet more exquisitely beautiful...When it reaches the top of the hill, the sparkling thing is divided into five or six branches, each one of which supplies one, two, or three 'long-toms.' There is an extra one, called the 'waste-ditch,' leading to the river, into which the water is shut off at night and on Sundays. This 'race' (another and peculiar name for it) has already cost the company more than five thousand dollars. They sell the water to others at the following rates: Those that have the first use of it pay ten per cent. upon all the gold that they take out. As the water runs off from their machine, (it now goes by the elegant name of 'tailings,') it is taken by a company lower down; and as it is not worth so much as when it was clear, the latter pay but seven per cent. If any others wish the 'tailings,' now still less valuable than at first, they pay four per cent. on all the gold which they take out, be it much or little. The water companies are constantly in trouble, and the arbitrations on that subject are very frequent...

Gold mining is Nature's great lottery scheme. A man may work in a claim for many months, and be poorer at the end of the time than when he commenced; or he may 'take out' thousands in a few hours. It is a mere matter of chance...

History Of California

by Theodore Hittell

(Volume III, p. 58, from *The California Gold Rush Diary of a German Sailor* by Adolphus Windeler, edited by Jackson, Berkeley, CA: Howell-North Books, 1969, p. 220)

...one of the most common methods of supplying...[water] and what may be called a characteristic of the river mining of California, was by means of a water-lifting wheel. At nearly every point along those rivers, where operations of any extent were carried on, great wheels, consisting of shafts, arms and cross boards and resembling the paddle-wheels of a steamboat, immersed just deep enough to be driven by the current, extended across the stream and revolved with more or less noise and clatter but untiring persistency. Attached to each of these wheels, and worked by it, was some kind of a contrivance for lifting water, usually a series of buckets on a belt, or chain with valves running through a trough, or a pump of large capacity; and every one of these contrivances supplied a long-tom and sometimes a sluice hundreds of feet long. Especially when the bed of the river was turned and it was found to be rich, wheels were frequent and sometimes as close together as they could be built.

California Emigrant Letters

by Walker D. Wyman

(New York: Bookman Associates, 1952, originally published in mid-19th century newspapers, pp. 138-139)

Diamond Springs, Feb. 1, 1851

In order to give you some idea of mining in this beautiful country you must imagine yourself a miner. Well, tie your blankets, knapsack fashion on your back; that accomplished, get your cradle next, not any of our modern cots (I think they call them) but the old fashioned cradles that you and I were rocked in; put that on top of your blankets; next a pick and shovel and pan, coffee pot, some provisions in the shape of flint bread and (the cause of scurvy) pork; straighten yourself, take your rifle in hand and off you go rejoicing! This is what we call 'prospecting,' you travel over some of the worst mountains I ever saw, so stupendous are they that it is the labor of extreme toil to ascend them. I must remark here that all the mines are in the mountains, on the water courses, ravines and gulches. You come to a ravine, take off your rigging, dig a hole from four to eight feet square and from three to six feet deep, you come to the bed rock where the gold is usually deposited, you find that your labor was all in vain. — You dig another hole and another, and find some gold, wash out some dirt as we call it; you find when you wash out about one hundred buckets full, perhaps five dollars, more commonly three; that will not pay; curse the gulch and your own hard fate, then your reflections are soothing in the extreme. You next gather some grass if you want to indulge a little in luxury, and make your bed; make a fire, eat your flint bread and pork, a little coffee without sugar, smoke your pipe and go to your blankets, where you will sleep sound. I can assure you gold digging makes a man sleep well. You awake in the morning, your head white, not with the frosts of many winters, but with the frost of a single night; jump up from your couch, shake yourself and you are dressed...Now you are determined to try the river, and attach yourself to some mere roving vagabonds you meet with, we call them the forlorn hope. Hope in this country loses all those beautiful charms upon which the mind so often and so fondly dwells. I digress: Well, you determine to turn the river, the company go to work, dig a race, which is the work of many days for many

hands. Next make your dam to turn the water from the bed of
the river, and when it is properly drained you go to work to dig
the bed of the stream, buoyed with hopes. You pick, shovel and
wash and get nothing. So it was on the bed of the Yuba, to my
own knowledge...twenty-one races were dug on this river, (Yuba)
by different companies who had some capital, and nineteen of
them paid nothing, the other two did not pay expenses... —
James Heren, Missouri Statesman, *May 16, 1851*

Scharmann's Overland Journey To California

by H.B. Scharmann

(Translated by Zimmermann and Zimmermann, Freeport, NY: Books for
Libraries Press, 1969, originally published in 1918, pp. 55-57, 73)

Because there have been so many misrepresentations of this
gold region, I shall attempt to describe it faithfully. Gold is
found just about where the mountains begin; there is nothing
in the valley. The mountains are almost perpendicular, and a
mountain a mile or more in height is a frequent sight. Nearer to
the river there are rocks which are sometimes fifty yards high, all
more or less steep, and often perpendicular. In the cracks of these
volcanic mountains the gold gravel is found. It has been washed
down from the mountains by heavy rainstorms. Wherever these
rocks do not exist, there is no gold. The gold hunter must creep
around among these rocks and has to scrape the gold gravel with
a hatchet or a shovel. Then he pours it into his sack and carries it
to the river. He has to be very careful to jump from one rock to
another in just the right way, otherwise he might easily break
his legs or his neck. When he has carried his sack up to the river,
one hundred to two hundred and fifty feet away, he must wash the
gravel...

Now the question arises, how much can a man earn by this dirty and exhausting work? When I arrived at the river, everything had been dug up and the best part of the gold was already gone...

...everyone was busy with wheel-barrow, shovel and hoe, digging into the gold-containing earth. Everyone carries two pails on his shoulder, suspended from a yoke. The yoke, pails and soil together weigh a hundred and twenty-five pounds. This burden is carried for two hundred and sixty-five paces up to the river. In order to spare myself the weight of the yoke and the pails, I filled a sack with the soil and carried it to the river where my younger son daily washed about two hundred and fifty pailfuls. This quantity was worth from twelve to fifteen dollars...

At the Feather River the gold diggers were occupied in building dams and digging canals. This was done to lead the river away from its main channel and to expose its original bed, so that they could get at the gold — a huge laborious task, but the hope of rich gain spurred them all on. The banks were now all dug up and stripped of their golden contents.

Audubon's Western Journal: 1849-1850

by John W. Audubon

(Glorieta, New Mexico: The Rio Grande Press, 1969, pp. 201-203)

[No date]...At times you may see two pits side by side, one man getting two ounces a day, and the other hardly two dollars: we heard of one instance of much greater disparity; two friends working next to each other found that at the end of the week, one had an ounce of gold, worth about twenty dollars, the other gold worth six thousand dollars. So it goes, and we shall all have to work hard...

*January 20th, 1850. Chinese Diggings...*The men began 'rocking' yesterday, one cradle, and get about a dollar an hour, but hope to get more when in the way of it. Those at work around us get an average of fourteen a day, and at times much more; then again a week's work is lost. The quantity of gold, so I am told by those who know more of it than I do, is very great, but so diffused that great labor is required to get it. The lottery of the whole affair is beyond belief. The richest gulches are supposed to be those on the river, the Tuolome [Tuolumne], or the creeks leading to the river. The pit, or piece of ground allotted to each man is sixteen feet square, thus having been settled by the diggers...Many is the week's work, the men say, when they do not get the price of their board, and again large amounts are found. One dividual told me he was getting two ounces a day, and gave his claim up, to join a company in digging out the bed of a river which they had drained off. He worked a month at the river scarcely making two dollars a day, while the man who bought his first place, had accumulated several thousands...

Gold was also found in veins of quartz ore which often extended away from narrow ravines (called gulches) in the mountains. This hard-rock or quartz mining was very difficult since the gold-bearing ore had to be crushed into powder to extract gold.

Crushing was first done with heavy stones but, by 1861, most quartz was pulverized by stamps (wooden shafts driven by machinery). Water and mercury were used in the stamping box to amalgamate the gold. In this process, the gold attached itself to the mercury to form an amalgam.

According to Phyllis Flanders Dorset in *The New Eldorado*, "After the day's work of mining was done and the miner had eaten his supper of beans and hardtack, he put the amalgam in a cast-iron retort (a special container) over his campfire. Under the heat of the fire the mercury vaporized, leaving a lump of native gold. This could be the best or worst moment of the day, since the day's take in dollars and cents was measured by how much the lump of gold weighed..."

Later, steam-powered stamp mills became part of the process. Then, in the mid-1860s, smelters were used to extract gold in large quantities. After the ore was crushed, it was heated to high temperatures in a large furnace and the gold was separated from other metals such as copper.

Eventually, by the turn of the century, a chemical cyanide process made it possible to extract one hundred percent of all precious metals in ore. Although the process is somewhat complicated, it basically involved soaking the ore in a weak solution of sodium cyanide, then running the solution through boxes of zinc shavings. Both gold (and silver) stuck to the zinc and could be separated from each other by heating.

Gold dust, nuggets and bars were weighed.

36

Silver Threads Among The Gold

by Phyllis Raybin Emert

The slogan of most prospectors was "gold is where you find it," and that could be anywhere. After the initial discoveries in California, gold seekers explored areas of Arizona, Utah, Montana, the Dakotas, Oregon, Washington, Colorado, Nevada, and even Alaska, in the last half of the 19th century, in hopes of making that one big strike.

Most Americans associated the phrases "strike it rich" and "instant wealth" with gold. But it was found that certain places were also rich in silver. Although silver was only worth one-tenth of gold, a large silver strike could prove to be very profitable.

There was one main problem. Silver was much harder to recognize than gold because it combined so easily with other metals and took on different colorations. Although silver was often referred to as "white metal," it was sometimes dark blue, black, yellow, green, dark red, or brown in color.

In fact, the only way to really identify silver was to test samples with nitric or hydrochloric acid, which was much too dangerous. So prospectors had to take ore samples to the local assay office to determine their silver content.

Silver was rarely found in creeks and riverbeds like gold. It often had to be dug out from below ground and extracted from the ore by the cyanide process or by amalgamation, which were similar processes to those used in extracting gold in hard-rock and quartz mining.

In the Washoe mountains of Western Nevada in the early 1850s, two brothers named Allen and Hosea Grosch were disappointed at the small amount of gold they had mined. They were

37

only making a few dollars a day and the gold flakes were trapped in a strange bluish-black sandy clay. The brothers took some samples and then moved on to try their luck at other claims.

After several years, and many samples and assays later, the two concluded that they had discovered a huge vein of silver. It was 1857 and since they had no money, they attempted to get financial backing to allow them to mine the silver. Not only were they unsuccessful, they were also incredibly unlucky.

Hosea axed himself in the foot and died of infection a short time later. Allen was on his way to California to meet a prospective developer when be became caught in a snowstorm on Donner Summit and froze to death.

A man named Henry Thomas Paige Comstock, who had been watching the Grosch cabin while they were gone, took over their claims, papers, and maps as soon as he heard of their deaths. But he couldn't figure out what they were so excited about. He and several partners continued to mine for gold.

One day in June of 1859, the miners began digging a reservoir to store spring water when they came upon a formation of gold that was unbelievably rich looking. They knew they had hit something big, so they traced off a claim and recorded it with the local blacksmith. The men called it the Ophir mine. There was plenty of gold, but the dark sandy clay contaminated the precious metal and lowered the price.

Within months, the men were offered thousands of dollars to sell their interests in the mine. Comstock figured the gold wouldn't last long, so he sold out for $11,000. The other men's shares were bought for $3,500, $7,000, $4,000, and $8,500.

What Comstock and his friends didn't know was that the pesky black substance was silver ore, and they had just sold the richest known silver deposit in United States history, collectively worth more than $60,000,000!

The eventual output of the Comstock Lode was fifty-five percent silver and forty-five percent gold. More than 30,000 people flocked to the area, once the secret was out, and the mining camp of Virginia City became a flourishing city.

Initially, it was the gold that the prospectors and developers were after. According to Gerald Higgs in *Lost Legends of the Silver State*, "The mine owners were having trouble extracting silver. It was not unusual for the mills to let $4,500 worth of silver drift, as tailings, into the Carson River, while they recovered $2,000 worth of gold. In 1861 alone, more than 750,000 pounds of silver ended up in the Carson Sink for lack of a reliable recovery method."

The mine's owners, with the help of chemists, finally developed a special chlorinating procedure as part of the amalgamation process which, when combined with mercury, resulted in amalgam. When heated, the mercury evaporated, leaving the silver.

A typical silver mine on the Comstock Lode was similar to a factory. A large building covered the main shaft entrance where machinists and carpenters worked. The mouth of the shaft was actually divided into four openings. Three contained cages for lowering and raising workers, ore, and supplies. Steel hoisting cables attached to the cages were powered by large engines and carefully controlled by engineers. The fourth opening contained the pumping equipment that pumped out water from the underground tunnels of the mine.

Men were lowered in the cages 1,500, 2,000, or even 3,000 feet underground to work in reinforced-timber tunnels where the ore was mined. The temperature was well over 100 degrees and the rock was hot enough to burn unprotected skin.

The risk of death and injury to miners was very high. Falls and cave-ins were common causes of death. Fires from candles which lit the tunnels were frequent. Even objects that accidentally fell down the shafts could kill men unlucky enough to be at the bottom. At first, hand drills and black powder were used to cut and blast holes in the rock. Around 1875, these were replaced by machine drills and dynamite, which were also very dangerous.

Great fortunes were made in the Comstock Lode, often called the "Treasures of the Ages." But the mines declined in the 1870s and were finally abandoned by the turn of the century.

The discovery and abundance of silver determined the economic development of Nevada. It wasn't a coincidence that, just as California became known as the Golden State when it was admitted to the Union in 1850, Nevada was called the Silver State when it was admitted in 1864. Other big silver strikes included the Hidden Treasure, the Eberhardt, and the Aurora mines in the 1860s, the Big Bonanza in 1873, and Tonopah in 1900.

As it had in Nevada, the discovery of silver played a significant role in the development of Colorado. But it was gold which first attracted large numbers of emigrants to Colorado, with major strikes reported in Cherry Creek (1858) and Central City (1859). These strikes first brought Horace and Augusta Tabor and their young son, Maxcy, from Maine. The Tabors tried working several claims but were only moderately successful at it. Most of their prosperity came in the late 1850s and early 1860s in opening and managing general stores in the Colorado gold mining camps.

Reminiscenses of Mrs. Augusta Tabor

from her original manuscript

(From Moynihan, *Augusta Tabor - A Pioneering Woman*, Evergreen, Colorado: Cordillera Press, Inc. 1988, pp. 123, 125)

After many hard days over steep, rocky hills, we camped where Cache Creek empties into the Arkansas. Here we pitched our tent and went to work in earnest. Mr. T. and Maxcy whipsawed some [boards], made two sluice boxes, sawed riffles from a log, made a ditch from the creek and commenced to work the bank away. Cleaning up the boxes every night, we found plenty of fine gold but more black sand, and being new at mining, knew no way to separate the gold from the sand, only with the slow process of lifting the iron sand with a small magnet...

The Tabors operated three stores, in upper California Gulch, Oro City and what eventually became the town of Leadville. They built a thriving business and Horace, at forty-five, was content to let others live the difficult life of a miner. It wasn't unusual, however, for Horace and Augusta to grubstake local prospectors (furnish provisions in exchange for a share of the profits if there were any).

Augusta Tabor as she looked in the 1870's.

One spring day in 1878, two down-on-their-luck miners named George Hook and August Rische took $17 worth of tools, supplies, and possibly a jug of whiskey from the Tabor's store and went prospecting. They agreed to give Horace 1/3 of their profits if they made a strike.

Within a month, Hook and Rische struck a vein of ore that was extremely rich in silver. It was called the Little Pittsburg mine and Horace Tabor eventually made millions from it. According to Betty Moynihan, "that annoying black sand which Augusta in the early years had tried so painstakingly to separate from the flakes of gold was, in fact, rich in silver-lead ore, which now interested all the miners."

Horace used earnings from the Little Pittsburg mine to purchase other silver claims in the Leadville area, including the very successful Chrysolite and Matchless mines. Now a multimillionaire, Tabor became involved in local and then state politics in Colorado, which had been admitted to the Union in 1876.

With silver strikes at Aspen, Creede, Leadville, and the San Juans, and those in Nevada and other areas, silver became so plentiful that its price began to fall. Over the last quarter of the 19th century, the price of silver fluctuated with whatever federal legislation was in effect. But not even an Act of Congress could stop its steady decline.

The death knell came for the silver mining industry in 1893 when the Sherman Silver Purchase Act was repealed. Silver plummeted to only fifty cents an ounce and silver ore became practically worthless. The mines went bankrupt and large numbers of men found themselves out of work. Even Horace Tabor's luck ran out, and he was left penniless.

The last nail on the silver coffin came in the Presidential election of 1896 where the candidates squared off in the battle of gold versus silver. Gold standard supporters of William McKinley were pitted against free silver advocate, William Jennings Bryan, who called for the free coinage of silver.

According to Robert L. Brown in his book, An Empire of Silver, "Sixteen ounces of silver were worth only about 11 dollars in 1896, while an ounce of gold would bring $20.67... There was a prevailing fear in Europe that if Bryan became President, America would try to pay off its debt in silver, which was not worth as much on the international market as in the United States Treasury."

It was the gold standard and William McKinley who won the election. As a result, a Gold Standard Act was adopted by the United States in 1900.

Even as silver mining declined, the average person's dream of instant wealth was still made of gold. Around the turn of the century, more of the yellow metal was discovered at Cripple Creek in Colorado, at Goldfield in Nevada, and in the Klondike region of Alaska. These new strikes, which stimulated local economies and promoted the development of new cities and towns, turned out to be the last of the real gold rushes.

Dick Roelofs, known as the "miracle miner of Cripple Creek" shows his discovery of pure gold crystals to Bert Carlton and Spencer Penrose. The geodes in the Cresson Mine brought in $1,200,000 in four weeks.

The Mining Camps:
From Shacks To Cities

Many of the settlements and mining camps which grew and flourished along with the discovery of gold and silver, faded into obscurity when these precious metals were eventually exhausted.

Some places such as Sacramento, San Francisco, Aspen, Denver, and Stockton continued to prosper and grow into large cities. Others like Virginia City and Tonopah have survived today only as small towns, whose main claim to fame was their association with the gold and silver rushes of the 19th century.

The Diaries of Peter Decker

by Peter Decker

(Edited by Giffen, Georgetown, California: The Talisman Press, 1966, pp. 154, 285)

...But for a description of *Sacramento City*. The City is situated on a level bottom or plain of the Sacramento at the confluence of the American Fork. The City is now a grove. The houses & tents being built among the brush & trees. The City is laid out regularly the streets crossing at right angles (American style). The population** being 4000. Houses are going up that were

**The population in Sacramento prior to 1848 was 250. It rose rapidly after the gold discovery and approached 20,000 at the end of 1849. In 1850 the city began to develop a permanent population. Many business buildings and residences were built that gave a substantial appearance to the community, and the population became more permanent and less transient.

shipped from the States. Many are also put up of lumber gotten here. But most houses are mere poles drove in the ground & muslin tacked on the sides & roof. Some roofs are covered with willow twigs. Most of the houses are tents and many live under trees in the suburbs especially Emigrants (which is the case with us). It is essentially a "Calico Town" & looks like a huge American Camp Meeting, most people living outdoors & the streets crowded with passers by, men from all nations, States & Races are mingled Enmasse here. 15 ships lay in port their riggings raising among the trees & bushes on the wharf. It is truly a business place & will some day be a great city. Lots now sell at from one to $300 & change hands daily. Rents are extravagant, one house $310 offered for. The Sacramento is 1/4 mile wide is the most beautiful stream I ever saw timbered on this side with White Oaks, on the other willows & beautiful little delicate foliaged trees entwined with grape vines looking rich indeed...

Scharmann's Overland Journey To California

by H.B. Scharmann

(Translated by Zimmermann and Zimmermann, Freeport, NY: Books for Libraries Press, 1969, originally published in 1918, p. 98)

May seventh. (1850)...Sacramento has rapidly grown into a city; it seems as though it had been built on the wings of the wind. There is scarcely any other place that is so lively and so full of trading, bargaining and usury. Every third house is a saloon and the owner uses every means in his power to attract guests. You hear music all about you and a few unhappy women are kept as a principal drawing card. People here talk about the gold region as though a man had only to stoop, in order to pick up the nuggets, and the papers publish the most absurd tales in order to attract new people...

The California Gold Rush Diary Of A German Sailor

by Adolphus Windeler

(Edited by Jackson, Berkeley, CA: Howell-North Books, 1969, pp. 35-36)

*Thursday morning Dec. 6th 1849...*San Francisco seems to be a poorly built town, small wooden houses, & mighty muddy streets. In some places it looks more like a Soldiers camp than a town. Small canvass tents cover the ground amongst the hills, but by all accounts there is plenty of money about, for our passengers, that have been ashore, say that doubloons, dollars & pieces of gold are everywhere to be seen. Plenty of money is made here, but boarding & lodging is dear in proportion from 12 to 28 $ a week. Days wages for mechanics from 12-16 $ per day. Houserent from 60 to 200 $ per Month. In the line of grub every thing is dear; potatoes 4 cents a piece, Salt port 35 $ p. brl. Sailors wages, 100-150 $ per month, night shift 100$, & a bottle Champagne 10 $...

Six Months In The Gold Mines

by E. Gould Buffum

(Edited by Caughey, The Ward Ritchie Press, 1959, originally published in 1850, from pages 99-101)

...the growth of San Francisco has been enormous...at least a thousand houses have been erected, of all sizes and forms. The hills around the town are now covered with buildings, and every spot of ground near the centre is occupied...the price of real estate has risen in proportion with the growth of the town, property being now fifty percent, higher than it was six months since. A lot on Portsmouth Square, which was purchased some three years ago for fifteen dollars, and sold last May for six thousand, was purchased a few days since for forty thousand dollars!

San Francisco possesses one of the most…magnificent harbours in the world; one in which the navies of all the maritime powers could ride at anchor in perfect safety. From its entrance to its head is a distance of about twenty miles, and branching from it are other large bays — San Pablo, and Suisun. The entrance to the harbour is guarded by lofty hills, about five thousand feet apart, and could be protected with the greatest of ease…Among the improvements in the town are several wharves, which have been completed within a short time past. The principal of these, the central wharf, built by a joint-stock company, extends into the harbour a distance of two hundred and ninety-two feet, and will, when completed, be twenty-one hundred feet in length, enabling vessels to lie abreast, and discharge their cargoes directly upon it…There are also two public schools in operation. Some ten or twelve steamboats are plying on the Sacramento and San Joaquin rivers, and the bay of San Francisco; so that travelling has ceased to be so disagreeable as it was when I went up the Sacramento in a little open boat…

According to Joann Levy, in *They Saw The Elephant*, "San Francisco was no longer a hamlet and California no longer a frontier. Its people no longer were only transient miners. Men were bankers and businessmen, lawyers and doctors, farmers and manufacturers. They intended to stay…"

Leisure Time And Social Life

One young miner wrote his father from California in 1849, "There is gold here, but it is the hardest work for a man to get hold of it that you ever saw..."

A miner's life was difficult, exhausting, back-breaking, and often unrewarding. Most prospectors were far from home and without their families. When it was time to relax and socialize, these lonely and bored men sought comfort and cheer in gambling and alcohol. If a miner didn't strike a vein of gold or silver, there was always a chance of instant wealth at the casinos and gambling halls. Too often, however, many a prospector lost everything he had with the throw of the dice or the turn of a card.

Although some camps sponsored dances, Independence Day celebrations and even church services and socials for those who were interested, it was gambling which continued twenty-four hours a day in some places. According to Robert Wallace in *The Miners*, "gambling was more prevalent in 19th Century silver and gold camps of the West than at any other time or place in American history."

Heavy drinking wasn't far behind gambling as a popular activity. Wallace noted that in 1880 more than 200,000 gallons of alcoholic beverages were brought in to Virginia City by railroad. Some miners drank a quart of whiskey each and every day.

The New Eldorado
The Story of Colorado's Gold and Silver Rushes

by Phyllis Flanders Dorset

(London, England: The MacMillan Company, 1970, p. 60)

"...Everyone carried his freshly mined gold dust in a small buckskin pouch as elsewhere coin and currency were carried...the merchants of 40-rod whiskey and deuces-wild poker got more than their fair share of the contents of the buckskin pouches. Saloons and gambling halls on Cherry Creek opened their doors with the sequential frequency of a stack of falling dominoes. Once open, they never closed. All day and all night the raucous cries of dealers drifted over the towns, and gambling fever was nearly as epidemic as gold fever..."

Audubon's Western Journal: 1849-1850

by John W. Audubon

(Glorieta, New Mexico: The Rio Grande Press, 1969, p. 187)

...We went into the 'Exchange Hotel,' which might better be called the 'Exchange of Blacklegs.' Such a crowd as the bar-room of this hotel presents nightly, cannot be found except where all nations meet. Cards were being played for stakes every where, and the crowd around added to the picture, which once seen is difficult to forget. The tall, raw-boned Westerner, bearded and moustached like his Mexican neighbor beside him, the broad-headed German and sallow Spaniard, French, Irish, Scotch, I know not how many nationalities are here represented. I saw even two Chilians with their cold, indifferent air, all mixing together, each man on his guard against his fellow man. The tight fitting jacket and flowing sarape touch each other, all blending into weirdness in the dim light of a few candles, would that I had time and opportunity to sketch some of the many scenes I beheld...

Diary Of A Forty-Niner

by Alfred T. Jackson

(Edited by Canfield, New York: Turtle Point Press, 1992, originally published in 1906, pp. 6, 10, 39, 122)

*June, 1850...*The place was full and running over with gamblers and miners, and the latter seemed to be trying to get rid of their money as fast as possible. At some of the tables they were playing for high stakes, as much as one hundred dollars on the turn of a card. Monte was the most popular game and while I was there 'Texas Bill' tapped one of the banks for two thousand dollars and won on the first pull. Then he took the dealer's seat and the banker quit until he could raise another stake.

There was a young French woman dealing twenty-one. She was as pretty as a picture. Began betting just to get near her and hear her talk. I lost seventy dollars and she did not notice me any more than she did the rest of the crowd...there were two or three thousand miners in town, the majority drinking, gambling and carousing. Woolen shirts and duck overalls are the fashion, and if you see anybody dressed up it's a sure thing he is either a gambler or a lawyer. What beats me is the craze the miners have for gambling. Every saloon has some sort of game running, and the big ones have a dozen. 'Monte,' 'Red and Black,' 'Chuck-a-Luck,' 'Twenty-One,' 'Rondo,' and 'Fortune Wheels' are the banking games, and they play poker and 'Brag' for big stakes. The fool miners work hard all the week and then lose their dust

51

at these games of chance. There does not seem to be much chance about them, for nobody ever heard a miner winning anything...

July 6, 1850. Been in town all day. The citizens had a celebration Friday, but it did not amount to much. Lawyer McConnell made a speech and another fellow read the Declaration of Independence. Then everybody fell into line, marched up and down the street, hurrahing and firing off pistols, and that was all there was to it. The town was jammed with outsiders and the hotels and restaurants ran short of grub. The saloons and gambling houses were chock-a-block and half the men in sight were full of rot-gut whiskey. Went in to see the pretty French woman, but could not get near the table she was dealing...

January 26, 1851. There was a lively time over at Selby Flat Wednesday night. The landlord gave a ball at the hotel. All the woman were there — seven of them —and about two hundred men. They had a fiddler — Mart Simonson; one of the best I ever heard. It was great sport for a while, but towards morning some of the men got too much gin aboard and a quarrel started about the right to dance with one of the Missouri girls. Pistols were drawn, the lights put out, at least a hundred shots fired; but, funny enough, only one man was hurt — San Creeley, who was hit in the leg. I went out through a window and did not wait to see the finish. It was too exciting for me...

The Role of Women

"Most gold rushers were single men, young, unhampered, free to pursue adventure..." declared Joann Levy in *They Saw The Elephant*. "Women decided that where men could go, they could go. Some women came alone, many more with husbands, fathers, brothers..."

Although few women participated in the early days of the gold and silver rushes, their numbers increased considerably with time. According to Robert Wallace in *The Miners*, "Women were so scarce in the mining frontier that any female was treated with a respect that sometimes verged on idolatry." A San Francisco census of 1847 listed 138 women among 459 residents. By the end of 1853, there were around 8,000 in the city by the bay.

Women found that they could earn money in several ways. Miners were willing to pay well– 1) for a good meal, 2) for clean clothes, and 3) to sleep in a clean bed. As a result, many women made small fortunes by running successful boarding houses, cooking large quantities of good food, and laundering the miners shirts and pants.

Several women had successful careers by dressing and living like a man. In the Nevadaville mining camp, the most popular saloon was "Mountain Charley" Forest's place. Drinking, swearing, and fighting were the main activities at Mountain Charley's, but few customers knew that Charley, the proprietor, was really the former housewife, Eliza Jane Forest.

Another person named Charley drove a stage coach for Wells, Fargo, and Company in the 1850s and 1860s. Charley Parkhurst was one of the most famous California stage drivers, who was known for his exceptional skill with horses and courage on the trail. It wasn't until Parkhurst's death in 1879 that it was discovered Charley was actually a woman.

The following excerpts deal with women in the gold and silver rushes and their actual experiences.

A Frontier Lady

by Sarah Royce

(Edited by Gabriel, New Haven, CT: Yale University Press, 1960, originally published in 1932, p. 83-84)

...A woman, the only one besides myself in the town... was a plain person who, with her husband, had come from one of the western states, and was acquainted only with country life. She was probably between thirty and thirty-five years of age... she called one day and in quite an exultant mood told me the man who kept the boarding house had offered her a hundred dollars a month to cook three meals a day for his boarders, that she was to do no dishwashing and was to have someone help her all the time she was cooking. She had been filling the place some days, and evidently felt that her prospect of making money was very enviable. Her husband, also, was highly pleased that his wife could earn so much. Again I saw nothing of her for some time, when again she called; this time much changed in style. Her hair was dressed in very youthful fashion; she wore a new gown with full trimmings, and seemed to feel in every way elevated. She came to tell me there was to be a ball at the public house in a few days; that several ladies who lived at different camps within a few miles, chiefly Hang-Town, were coming; and she came to say that I might expect an invitation as they would like very much to have me come. I laughingly declined, as being no dancer, and entirely unfitted to adorn any such scene…it gave me a glimpse of the ease with which the homeliest if not the oldest, might become a 'belle' in those early days, if she only had the ambition; and was willing to accept the honor, in the offered way.

California Emigrant Letters

by Walker D. Wyman

(New York: Bookman Associates, 1952, originally published in mid-19th century newspapers, pp. 147-148)

We have now been keeping house three weeks. I have ten boarders, two of which we board for the rent. We have one hundred and eighty-nine dollars per week for the whole. We think we can make seventy-five of it clear of all expenses, but I assure you I have to work mighty hard — I have to do all my cooking by a very small fire place, no oven, bake all my pies and bread in a dutch oven, have one small room about 14 feet square, and a little back room we use for a store room.about as large as a piece of chalk. Then we have an open chamber over the whole, divided off by a cloth…

Mrs. H — took some ironing to do, and what time I had I helped and made seven dollars in as many hours…I don't care to go into a house until I get ready to go home; not that I am homesick, but it is nothing but gold, gold — no social feelings — and I want to get my part and go where my eyes can rest upon some green things. — *A Boarding House Keeper, formerly of Portland, Maine, to her children — Portland* Advertiser, *quoted by Missouri* Republican, *Oct. 6, 1849*

They Saw The Elephant

by Joann Levy

(Hamden, CT: Archon Books, 1990, pp. 102, 114)

Mrs. McKinney had a nephew who went to California in 1849, and she told me of the wonderful tales of the abundance of gold that she had heard; 'that they kept flour-scoops to scoop the gold out of the barrels that they kept it in, and that you could soon get all you needed for the rest of your life. And as for a woman, if she could cook at all, she could get $16.00 per week for each man that she cooked for, and the only cooking required to be done was just to boil meat and potatoes and serve them on a big chip of wood, instead of a plate, and the boarder furnished the provisions.' I began at once to figure up in my mind how many men I could cook for, if there should be no better way of making money. — *Margaret Frink, 1850*

I determined to set up a rival hotel. So I bought two boards from a precious pile belonging to a man who was building the second wooded house in town. With my own hands I chopped stakes, drove them into the ground, and set up my table. I bought provisions at a neighboring store, and when my husband came back at night he found, mid the weird light of the pine torches, twenty miners eating at my table. Each man as he rose put a dollar in my hand and said I might count him as a permanent customer. I called my hotel 'El Dorado.' — *Luzena Stanley Wilson, Nevada City, 1850*

Law And Order —Life And Death

In the early days of the gold and silver rushes, there was little serious crime in the mining camps. The prospectors made their own laws and they were harsh and swift, ranging from execution by hanging, to public whippings, to amputation of the ears and exile from the mining camps. When the rare crime did occur, the offender might be arrested, tried, sentenced and hung, all in one afternoon. Law and order was maintained because most miners believed they had an equal chance to strike it rich and felt no need to steal from others.

As time passed and the population of the mining camps increased, so did the incidence of crime in mining communities. More miners competed against each other for claims, so it was more difficult to strike it rich. With the coming of professional gambling and the prevalence of heavy drinking, crime rates rose. The 'Lynch Law' mentality became more commonplace and in some areas, vigilante committees of unauthorized citizens often-times took matters into their own hands.

In general, however, responsible miners set up governing committees, known as mining districts, to police themselves, as well as to make laws regulating mining claims. These laws determined claim boundaries and requirements, registration and buying and selling procedures; provided punishment for claim-jumping and hearings to settle claim disputes. When these areas became official territories, and eventually achieved statehood, the mining districts formed the basis for future civil and criminal justice systems and provided the framework for organized local and state governments.

The following excerpts deal with law and order, life, death, and violence in the gold and silver mining communities.

Dreams To Dust
A Diary Of The California Gold Rush 1849-1850

by Charles Ross Parke

(Edited by Davis. Lincoln, Nebraska: University of Nebraska Press, 1989, p. 85)

Sept. 8, 1849... The 'miner's laws' are swift and certain in their execution. Men seldom steal even a pick or shovel here, the penalty being death without delay, with priest and preacher many miles away and no disposition to hunt him up. No 'great criminal lawyer' is allowed to humbug twelve dough men in this country, thereby creating a hope of escape in some would-be assassin. When caught in the act, *up they go*, and that's the end of it.

A Frontier Lady

by Sarah Royce

(Edited by Gabriel, New Haven, CT: Yale University Press, 1960, originally published in 1932, pp. 81-82)

... In almost every mining camp there was enough of the element of order, to control, or very much influence, the opposite forces. These facts soon became apparent to me, and ere long, I felt as secure in my tent with the curtain tied in front, as I had formerly felt with locked and bolted doors. There was, of course, the other element as elsewhere; but they themselves knew that it was safer for law and order to govern; and, with a few desperate exceptions were willing, to let the lovers of order enjoy their rights and wield their influence...

California Emigrant Letters

by Walker D. Wyman

(New York: Bookman Associates, 1952, originally published in mid-19th century newspapers, pp. 174-175)

Colloma, Aug. 15, 1849

The country is in a quiet condition, and property and persons are entirely safe. We hear of no murders or robbing, and thieving is very rare. Houses and whole Towns are built by sitting up posts and weatherboarding and roofing... as there is nothing to ward off the sun and dust, till the rainy season comes and by then all expect to be rich or at home. Under these shells splendid stores and groceries are spread out and merchandise lays scattered around out doors in day and night, with the Indian, African, Chinese, Chilean and all other races passing to and fro. No man scarcely steals when on his discovery he knows he will swing, and when at the same time he can go to the nearest rivulet and pick up perhaps $16 per day, without risk. And from the same easy acquisition, any man though an entire stranger can go to a merchant and buy plenty of goods on credit. Honor and that alone is confided in him, and it is the most honest country I ever knew in my life... And single individuals ramble about and travel the roads day and night with more or less money (for all have money here) unarmed and unhurt. — *"Old Boone," Alta California, quoted by Missouri Statesman, Octo. 26, 1849*

The Diaries of Peter Decker

by Peter Decker

(Edited by Giffen, Georgetown, California: The Talisman Press, 1966, p. 321-322)

Letter from James G. Canfield to Columbus, *Ohio State Journal,* August, 1849

The mines are the most quiet places I ever saw. A man is as safe here as he would be locked up in a room at home. They deal very severely with a man for stealing or robbing in this country. For stealing any small article they tie him to a tree and whip him severely, and then cut off both ears and let him go. For robbing they whip in the morning and hang him in the evening. For murder they hang him on the first tree. The first night I arrived in the diggings I slept under the limbs of a tree where three men were hung for robbery a few weeks ago. A man can have any amount of valuable property by a tree or by the road side — go off and be gone for days, and return and find everything as he left it. In the towns the streets are full of property and provisions of all kinds, and they do not pretend to watch them, day and night, and they are as safe as they would be in the States under strong locks and bolts. There is no more danger in California than in the streets of Columbus. So you need not give you an uneasiness on that score.

The Miners

by Robert Wallace

(Alexandria, Virginia: Time-Life Books, 1976, p. 37)

With the exception of the discoverer of a new gold field a miner could stake only one claim in the district. The discoverer got two. In very rich ground, the basic claim size might be as small as 10 feet square; while in leaner areas, it might be as large as 100 feet. On narrow creeks, the placer claim might extend from bank to bank; on wider watercourses, it might go only to the thread or center of the channel, with room for access and work on one bank. Every claim had to be boldly marked, and the date, location and claimant's name had to be filed with the district recorder, who was often a saloonkeeper or merchant. Clarity, not elegance, was all that was required in marking the claim stakes. For example, one early claim notice warned all comers, 'CLAME NOTISE — Jim Brown of Missoury takes this ground; jumpers will be shot.'

Having staked a claim, a man was obliged to work on it — typically, at least one day in three — to retain title. If he did not show up for 10 days or two weeks, the claim would be taken by someone else. No man could dump waste earth or rock onto his neighbor's claim or interfere with the general water supply. A placer miner had free use of the river as it passed through his claim, but — in one rule that was often flouted — could not divert or impound the flow at the expense of his downsteam colleagues. Naturally, claims could be bought and sold at will, but to prevent fraud or coercion, each transaction had to be witnessed by at least two and sometimes five disinterested men.

Poem by Adolphus Windeler

Life in California:
Bitter is the life of a miner,
who has no claim what pays,
who never wins a Shiner;
And works six out of seven days.
Who prospects many a panful,
And the color never sees,
drinks water by the canful,
And sleeps beneath the trees.
Who sinks oft holes twelve feet,
& pitching off so very steep
finds the bedrock hard & sound;
which every way he takes a peep,
no gold is to be found.
And washes buckets many,
of dirt he thinks will pay.
But gold he can't get any,
Although 'tis sticky clay.'
His food is bread & butter,
if Storekeepers will trust,
And often does he mutter,
A curse at his hard crust.
And for a change of living
he boils a lot of beans,
the hills in Spring are giving
him California greens.
But never mind old fellow,
Keep on yet for a while
try, work another 'hollow,'
And you may find your 'pile.'

Suggestions for Further Reading

Note: The passages excerpted in this book from other sources are noted at the beginning of each section

Brown, Robert L. *An Empire of Silver.* Denver, Colorado: Sundance Publishers Limited, 1984.

Higgs, Gerald B. *Lost Legends of the Silver State.* Salt Lake City, Utah: Western Epics, Inc. 1976.

Paher, Stanley W. *Tonopah – Silver Camp of Nevada.* Las Vegas, Nevada: Nevada Publications, 1978.

Rohrbough, Malcolm J. *Aspen – The History of a Silver Mining Town 1879-1893.* Oxford University Press, 1986.

Wallace, Robert. *The Miners.* Alexandria, Virginia: Time-Life Books, 1976.

About the Editor

Phyllis Raybin Emert has a B.A. degree in Political Science from the State University of New York at Stony Brook and an M.A. degree in Political Science/Public Administration from Penn State.

A free lance writer for nearly twenty years, this is her thirty-first published book. She has written on a variety of subjects—from airplanes, animals, and automobiles, to pretzels, sports heroes, and unsolved mysteries. Ms. Emert is also the editor of and wrote the introductory essays for Discovery Enterprises, Ltd.'s *Women in the Civil War: Warriors, Patriots, Nurses and Spies,* also in this Perspectives on History Series.